MENTAL ILLNESS

Not all in the mind

A **Mental Health Project**
publication

Edited by Patrick Holford

About the
Mental Health Project

The Mental Health Project is a voluntary action group, open to all, set up and supported by the Institute for Optimum Nutrition, an independent educational charity. The Mental Health Project is entirely supported by donations of time and money. It exists to inform the public about the role of nutrition in mental health, to promote the nutrition connection to health professionals, policy makers and sufferers, and to provide resources to encourage more research and implementation of nutritional strategies to reduce mental suffering.

Meetings of the Mental Health Project, which are held regularly at ION, Blades Court, Deodar Road, Putney, London SW15 2NU, are open to anyone who wishes to further these aims. Should you wish to attend please call ION on 0181-877 9993.

This book is the accumulated effort of a number of volunteers who have helped research, write, edit, produce, fund and distribute it. Our special thanks go to the main contributors - Katherine Monbiot, Graeme Wilson, Kirsten Blaikie, Karen Chung, Tuula Tuormaa and Patrick Holford; and to Liz, Anna, David and John for allowing us to tell their stories; and to Sue, Jan and many others for their help.

You can support the Mental Health Project by buying as many copies as you wish and distributing them to your doctor, MP, journalists, sufferers, carers and any other people who may benefit directly or indirectly from this information.

To obtain more copies please complete the card at the end of the book.

The current approach to mental health problems mainly involves drug therapy or psychotherapy. We believe, and present the evidence for our belief in this book, that a significant proportion of mentally unwell people do not need drugs, nor respond well to psychotherapy because the primary cause of their problem is neither a lack of drugs nor a lack of psychological insight or support, but a chemical imbalance that affects how they think and feel, brought on by years of inadequate nutrition and exposure to pollutants and environmental toxins.

To some this idea may seem strange, almost too simplistic. Yet any intelligent person can recognise that our diets have changed fundamentally in the last 100 years, as too has the air we breathe, the water we drink and our total environment. When one considers that the body and brain are entirely made from molecules derived from food, air and water, and that simple molecules like alcohol can fundamentally affect the brain, isn't it rather unlikely that changes in diet and the environment haven't affected mental health?

Of course, most people adapt well, but some, perhaps those most short-changed in nutrition, pollution, love, support or inherited resilience, go over the edge and become mentally unwell. Neither drugs nor psychotherapy have an impressive success rate. After 30 years of positive research and good results we believe that the time has come for another option, nutrition counselling, to be made widely available to those with mental health problems.

This book is dedicated to those who are searching for another piece to the jigsaw of mental health in the hope that they will find a missing piece that makes all the difference.

Foreword

The belief that behaviour is mainly or even wholly determined by social factors is so strongly entrenched in modern society that it ihas only recently been questioned. By social factors we mean those influences reaching us_via our senses. This belief largely determines our present policies towards various forms of mental illness, and even political problems in general. Yet it is dangerously mistaken. Our ancestor many millenia ago who discovered the behaviour - and thought-modifying effects of alcohol was unwittingly demonstrating that non-social factors which influence brain chemistry can also be critically important. The modern 'drugs scene' teaches the same lesson, but this lesson is still largely unlearnt in psychiatry, criminology, and the social sciences despite, paradoxically, the widespread use of neuroleptic drugs in psychiatry.

These neglected non-social factors include certain pharmaceutical drugs, faulty nutrition and exposure to antinutrients and neurotoxins, some of which are present as environmental pollutants.

I therefore welcome the Mental Health Project with its emphasis on the need for a more holistic approach to disordered mentation and behaviour in our turbulent society. This does not of course mean that social factors are unimportant, but rather they are only part of the picture.

Professor Derek Bryce-Smith PhD, DSc, CChem, FRSC.

The idea that dietary and environmental chemical factors may contribute to explaining many problems in mental functioning, emotional stability and behaviour is one which our existing mental health services are loathe to countenance. It is easier to postulate in substantial psychological causes and throw hastily prescribed drugs at them than to apply existing knowledge to more rational problem solving.

Sufferers seeking to discover whether, and, if so, how, their chemical environment broadly conceived, may be wrecking their mental health and what they can do about it, must work out their own salvation. The Institute for Optimum Nutrition, with this Mental Health Project, provides an excellent starting point for their enquiries.

Dr Vicky Rippere Ph.D, MPhil, CPsychol, FBPsS

Contents

PART ONE

What is Mental Illness?

Before discussing in this book certain factors which relate to mental illness, it is important to understand what we mean by this term. It is often used by layman and specialist alike as an identity tag with no apparent clear–cut definition or understanding.

In fact, the UK Mental Health Act of 1983 contains no definition. Instead it states, 'In practice the decision as to whether a person is mentally ill is a clinical one and the expression invariably has to be defined by reference to what the doctor says it means in a particular case rather than to any precise legal criteria.'

Blacks Medical Dictionary defines it as, 'problems of feeling, thinking and behaving may be regarded as a mental illness if they become excessive for the particular individual in relation to the difficulties experienced.'

What we commonly understand by the term 'mental illness' is a state of being that falls short of what we consider normal or acceptable. We have all experienced some degree of this. We become unhappy for no apparent reason, or find ourselves reacting explosively to the smallest of stimuli. We hear voices which just won't go away, or feel that we can't go on any more.

In practice, what tends to happen is that a person who continuously suffers from less than normal mental states is labelled depressed, manic–depressive, schizophrenic or with some other mental disorder. He may then carry this label for life, and be tagged as a less than normal human being. Such labels do nothing of actual benefit for the individual, so in defining what we mean by mental illness it is important to avoid a labelling which in itself could contribute to the individual's mental turmoil.

It might therefore be more useful to define our terms in reference to the concept of mental health. If a good state of mental health refers to a condition of feeling stable and satisfied that one is coping adequately with the problems of day to day living, then a mental health problem would refer to a condition where one is NOT coping, where a person is unhappy a lot of the time, frequently feels distressed and is unnaturally and frequently afraid.

With that in mind, for the purposes of this book we will refer to mental illness as being a state of mind in which one is unable to cope with some aspect of life to the point where one's ability to lead a fulfilling life is seriously impaired.

Mental Health Problems – Who Suffers?

Mental health problems are as common as heart disease, three times more common than cancer and five times more common than mental handicap. Official figures suggest that 6 million people are sufferers at any one time 1. In the course of a year 12 million adults attending GP surgeries have symptoms of mental health problems. Between 1985 and 1990 the number of children up to the age of 14 seen by psychiatric services has approximately doubled 2. In fact out of 100 people that you know up to 20 will be affected at any given time. Whilst 6 out of 10 people with mental health problems will be formally identified and receiving treatment, whether or not effective, an estimated 4 out of 10 are not receiving the help that they need.

As unwelcome as the thought may be, any one of us is a potential sufferer of a mental health problem. We are all subject to a greater or lesser degree to the stresses and strains of daily life, which, for many people may be in addition to a much deeper source of stress or unhappiness coming from a particularly difficult past or present experience. The vast majority (80%) of sufferers are labelled as having anxiety states, depression or stress–related disorders with the remaining 20% being labelled as having alcohol and drug dependency, dementia, personality and psychotic disorders such as schizophrenia 1.

With more than 4 in 10 mentally ill people being considered seriously at risk and therefore in need of specialist treatment, the cost of caring for sufferers is vast. Despite the fact that the numbers of long–stay hospital patients halved during the 1980s, more people are occupying beds for shorter periods or are using out–patient services. In 1991 the official cost of treating those with mental health problems was £3.15 billion - 9% of the total NHS expenditure 1. However, many other costs are also incurred, with industry losing £6.2 billion and sickness and invalidity benefit costing a further £1.14 billion a year. None of these figures take into account the cost of informal care taking place in the home, estimated at £1.16 billion and complicated by the fact that 76% of those looked after suffer from physical health problems in addition to mental problems. The total cost to the nation of mental illness exceeds £10 billion, or approximately £200 per member of the population.per year 1.

The effects of social deprivation on mental health cannot be disputed. Suicide rates are 11 times higher among the unemployed and 53 people per thousand are being admitted to psychiatric hospitals from deprived areas as opposed to 19 per thousand as a national average 1. However, this still begs the question as to why some people seem to cope reasonably well with a given situation while others will start to manifest the symptoms of mental illness. The answer to this is, of course, not cut and dried, but an increasing body of evidence points to one of the underlying causes of mental health problems being an actual physical or chemical imbalance in the body .

Where Can You Get Help?

For those coping with mental health problems, and those caring for people with such problems, help can be difficult to find. However, there is help at hand if you know where to look.

Initially, most people go to their GP but it is not always easy for those with mental health problems to recognise that there is a problem that needs addressing. Too often sufferers have a complete breakdown and end up in hospital. Either way the sufferer will be referred to a specialist, often with a long waiting list, during which time they may become more and more unstable. For more pronounced mental health problems the prescription is drugs, often given by injection and monitored through the hospital. Once the person leaves hospital they should be assigned a key worker, a social worker or community nurse who is there to help with problems that arise with their drugs, benefit forms or accommodation.

Socialising and interacting with others facing similar mental health problems is a great help to recovery. The 'drop in centres' run by MIND or Priority Care Units and Trusts such as the Blackthorn Trust provide that help in the form of art and music therapy, gardening experience and even cookery. The carers and relatives also need support. When one member of the family is mentally unwell it places a strain on the whole family. Most towns have support groups run by the Carers National Association, the Manic Depression Fellowship and the National Schizophrenia Association.

There is a growing awareness of the benefits gained from complementary medicine, especially from nutritional counselling. The Institute for Optimum Nutrition has helped many people with depression, manic depression and schizophrenia. Nutrition counselling can usually alleviate and sometimes cure mental health problems. Nutrition counsellors can now be found in most parts of the country (see page 30).

A list of these supporting organisations and their addresses and phone number is given on the following page.

Alzheimers Disease Society
Gorsan House, 10, Greencoat Place
London SW1 1PH Tel: 0171 306 0606

The British Association of Counselling
1 Regent Place, Rugby, Warks, CV21 2PJ Tel: 01788 578328

Blackthorn Trust Centre
St. Andrews Road, Maidstone, Kent, ME16 9AN Tel: 01622 726128

Citizens Commission for Human Rights
PO Box 188, East Grinstead, West Sussex RH19 2FL Tel:01342 313926

Carers National Association
20–25, Glasshouse Yard, London, EC1A 4JS Tel: 0171 490 8818

Hyperactive Children's Support Group
71 Whyke Lane, Chichester, West Sussex
PO19 2LD SAE please.

Institute for Optimum Nutrition
Blades Court, Deodar Road, London SW15 2NU Tel: 0181 877 9993

Manic Depression Fellowship
8–10 High Street, Kingston–on–Thames,
Surrey, KT1 1EY Tel: 0181 974 6550

The Maudsley Hospital
Denmark Hill, Camberwell, London SE5 8AZ Tel: 0171 703 6333

The Mental Health Foundation
37 Mortimer Street, London, W1N 7RJ Tel: 0171 580 0145

MIND
22 Harley Street, London, W1N 2ED Tel: 0171 637 0741

National Schizophrenia Fellowship
28 Castle Street, Kingston–on–Thames,
Surrey, KT1 1SS Tel: 0181 547 3837

SANE
2nd Floor, 199–205 Old Marylebone Road,
London, NW1 5QP Tel: 0171 724 6520

The Schizophrenia Association of Great Britain
International Schizophrenia Centre,
Bryn Hyfryd, The Crescent, Bangor,
Gwynnedd, LL57 2AG Tel: 01248 354048

PART TWO

Mental Health –
The Nutrition Connection

*Monica had a long history of mental illness. She had spent most of
her life on drugs and had even been given a lobotomy. While these
treatments sedated her she continually suffered from depression and
occasional 'highs'. At the age of 70 she consulted a nutrition
counsellor. At this point she was on two drugs - Depixol injections
and Flupenthixol. She had side-effects from the drugs, as well as high
blood pressure. Her nutrition counsellor identified nutritional
deficiencies. As soon as these were corrected the depression lifted. She
was able to stop one drug and halve the dose of Depixol. With this she
continued to improve and had reduced drug side-effects. Her blood
pressure stabilised so that she stopped medication for this too. She no
longer has 'highs', nor depression and, for the first time in as long as
she remembers, feels normal.*

Quantum leaps in our understanding about how thoughts and
feelings become disordered have been made in the last 50 years.
The mysteries of the human brain are being unravelled as we
identify the functions of different aspects of the brain, and how brain
cells, called *neurons*, communicate with each other with electrical and
chemical messages. The chemical messengers are called *neurotransmitters*
and it is well established that imbalances in these neurotransmitters can
result in depression, hallucinations, anxiety, insomnia, blank mind,
learning difficulties, poor impulse control and other mental health
problems [3].

While some mental health problems may have little to do with the
hardware, instead requiring support and guidance from friends and
counsellors, there is little doubt that many people with mental health
problems do have real chemical imbalances that predispose them to
becoming depressed, anxious or confused.

Until recently the only available method of helping to balance the
chemistry of the brain was through a variety of drugs which tend to
dampen emotional and mental activity, and, in many cases, have
undesirable side-effects including addiction. Only when scientists started
to examine what the brain and nervous system was actually made of did
the importance of nutrition - the food you eat - become apparent.

The brain is made entirely out of molecules derived from food. It
concentrates large amounts of complex essential fats, vitamins, minerals,

proteins and other nutrients. No less than sixty per cent of all nutrients passed from the mother to the developing infant during pregnancy are used by the brain for its development. Even in a fully grown adult, about thirty per cent of all energy derived from food is used by the brain. Human beings have a brain that is ten times heavier in relation to body weight than almost every other animal and, we have learnt, are totally dependent on a diet rich in nutrients for mental and emotional health.

With these discoveries medical researchers started to investigate whether some mental health problems could be corrected by giving certain nutrients. This approach was called orthomolecular medicine, meaning medicine that gives the body the right (ortho) molecules to maintain health. Two psychiatrists in Canada, Dr Abram Hoffer and Dr Humphrey Osmond, started to report amazing recoveries in patients labelled as schizophrenic, using large amounts of vitamins and minerals 4. An American doctor and biochemist, Dr Carl Pfeiffer, identified types of mental illness that could be corrected by specific diets and nutrients 5. He identified zinc deficiency as a cause of mental illness and developed nutritional approaches for correcting neurotransmitter imbalances. He believed that, if there was a drug that could affect mental health, then the right intake of nutrients could achieve the same result, or better, without the side effects.

Since the pioneering research of the 60s, nutrition has been identified as a major factor in hyperactivity, learning difficulties, delinquent behaviour, depression, anxiety, schizophrenia, insomnia, memory loss, anorexia – in fact almost every known type of mental health problem has been positively helped by nutritional therapy 6.

Nutritional deficiencies are not simply the result of eating a bad diet. Modern man is exposed to many chemicals which interfere with how the nutrients from food work. These are called anti–nutrients and include certain kinds of food additives, household chemicals, drugs and inhaled pollutants from smoking, exhaust and industrial pollution. For example, lead in petrol and cadmium in cigarettes are two anti–nutrients that accumulate in the brain and affect behaviour and mood 7. Since the 1940s over 6,500 totally new, man–made chemicals have been introduced into our food and homes 8.

Taking in too few beneficial nutrients and too many harmful anti–nutrients can easily affect the level and balance of both physical and mental energy. Without sufficient energy it is hard to concentrate and hard to cope with the stresses and demands of modern living. This often leads to the over–consumption of stimulants such as sugar, tea, coffee, cigarettes, chocolate and stimulant drugs in an attempt to boost energy. However, in the long run, stimulants deplete energy, as well as predisposing the user to states of anxiety and hyperactivity. The

over–consumption of stimulants is therefore another contributory factor that leads to mental and emotional imbalance. Conversely, over–stimulation as experienced in states of anxiety, may lead to the use of depressants including alcohol and tranquillizer drugs.

As well as identifying the role of nutrients, anti–nutrients, stimulants and depressants in mental health, research over the last 30 years has proven the very real existence of food allergies or intolerances that result in mental and emotional symptoms [9].

The combination of any of the following: sub–optimum nutrition, exposure to anti–nutrients, over–use of sugar, stimulants and depressants, and food allergies or intolerances – is now thought to be a very real contributor to mental and emotional health problems. The correction of these factors often results in substantial improvement. Let's now examine the evidence for each factor and the practical advice that is likely to make a difference.

Sugar and Stimulants

David was diagnosed as suffering from schizophrenia at the age of 20, having suffered from acute depression, paranoia and extreme mental confusion. He was also seeing and hearing things. He was put on the drug Stelazine which calmed him down, but he felt disoriented and couldn't go back to college or relate with friends and family in a normal way. He went to see a nutrition counsellor who identified that he was chronically deficient in vitamin B6 and zinc and had glucose intolerance. Within days of adding B6 and zinc supplements, changing his diet and avoiding sugar, coffee and alcohol he became symptom free. He was able to stop taking Stelazine and is now doing very well at University without any recurrence of his previous mental health problems.

The desire to eat sweet foods is prevalent in most societies all over the world. Sugar comes in many forms, from its most natural and wholesome packaging in fresh fruit to pure white table sugar, one of its most refined manifestations. Alcohol usually also contains a high sugar content. Stimulants are likewise universally popular. Nicotine in cigarettes and caffeine from tea, coffee, cocoa, cola drinks and chocolate are part of many people's daily routine. Most people would consider consumption of one or more of these as a normal part of everyday life. So why should there be a cause for concern? Just because everybody does it doesn't mean it's OK. Evidence is accumulating that excess sugar and stimulants has a disturbing effect on mental and emotional health by disrupting the balance of blood sugar, the brain's fuel.

There is a very important balancing act operating in the body by which a stable glucose or blood sugar level is maintained in the bloodstream. This is crucial in providing us with an even supply of energy for both body and mind. The brain relies completely on a continuous supply of glucose from the blood in order to work properly, with 30 per cent of available glucose being used as brain fuel. When glucose drops too low the brain immediately suffers, resulting in symptoms ranging from weakness, fatigue, faintness, dizziness, nervousness, irritability and trembling to anxiety, depression, forgetfulness, disruptive outbursts, confusion, difficulty concentrating, palpitations and blackouts. The term used to describe this difficulty with glucose control is glucose intolerance or hypoglycemia. It is estimated that as many as 1 in 4 people suffer from symptoms of glucose intolerance. Studies in prisons have found almost all offenders to have glucose intolerance [10]. Among those with mental health problems it is likely that the majority have glucose intolerance as

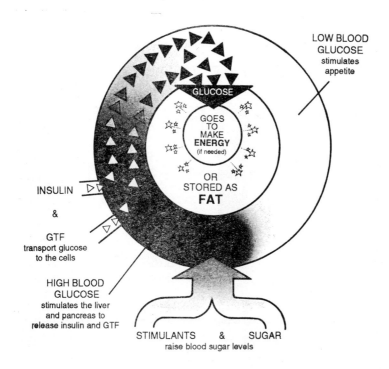

LOW BLOOD
GLUCOSE
stimulates
appetite

GLUCOSE

GOES
TO
MAKE
ENERGY
(if needed)

OR
STORED AS
FAT

INSULIN

&

GTF
transport glucose
to the cells

HIGH BLOOD
GLUCOSE
stimulates the liver
and pancreas to
release insulin and GTF

STIMULANTS & SUGAR
raise blood sugar levels

an underlying tendency. A high intake of stimulants such as tea, coffee, sugar and cigarettes is frequently reported in mental institutions.

It is the carbohydrate component in our diet which is digested and absorbed into the bloodstream as glucose. The pancreas responds to the arrival of the glucose into the blood by producing insulin which aids the transport of glucose into body cells for energy production, thereby stabilising blood glucose levels. When blood glucose drops significantly, for example after a long time without food, the adrenal glands are stimulated to release adrenaline and other hormones which act to normalise blood glucose levels by releasing glucose from the liver. Unfortunately, this elegant mechanism can easily be disturbed by the excessive use of sugar and stimulants, which trigger adrenaline release, with symptoms of glucose intolerance as a likely outcome. When sugary foods, alcohol or other highly refined carbohydrates are consumed frequently, the pancreas begins to over-react by producing too much insulin so that glucose drops below its optimum level. The adrenals become exhausted after a while in its continuous attempts to boost blood glucose. Symptoms of glucose intolerance set in and a vicious cycle is created as more sugar is craved to relieve the symptoms. Caffeine and

15

Which Foods Raise Blood Sugar Levels?
• The Glyceamic Index of Foods •
The foods with the great effect on blood sugar have the highest score.

	HIGH (55+) Limit	LOW (0-54) Increase		HIGH (55+) Limit	LOW (0-54) Increase
Sugars			**Cereals**		
Glucose	100		Puffed rice	90	
Maltose	100		Cornflakes	80	
Lucozade	95		Weetabix	75	
Honey	87		Shredded wheat	67	
Mars Bar	68		Muesli	66	
Sucrose (sugar)	59		All–Bran		52
Fructose		20	Porridge oats		49
			Rice bran		19
Fruit			**Pulses**		
Watermelon	72		Baked beans (no sugar)		40
Raisins	64		Butter beans		36
Bananas	62		Chick peas		36
Orange juice		46	Blackeye beans		33
Grapes		44	Haricot beans		31
Oranges		40	Kidney beans		29
Apples		39	Lentils		29
Apple juice		37	Soya beans		15
Breads			**Dairy Products**		
French baguette	95		Yoghurt		36
Rice cakes	82		Whole milk		34
Brown bread	69		Skimmed milk		32
White bread	69				
Ryvita	69		**Vegetables (cooked)**		
Oat cakes		54	Parsnips	97	
Rye whole grain (pumpernickel)		49	Carrots	92	
			Instant potato	80	
Grain Products			New potato	70	
White rice	72		Beetroot	64	
Brown rice	66		Peas		51
Brown rice pasta	92		Yam		51
Pastry	59		Sweet potato		48
Digestive biscuits	59		Sweetcorn		48
White spaghetti		50			
Wholemeal spaghetti		42			
Barley		22			

nicotine work in a similar way. They encourage glucose intolerance by their stimulant effect on the adrenals, creating a glucose high, followed by a sharp drop, followed by the next craving for a cigarette or a cup of coffee. In time the adrenals become depleted, glucose intolerance becomes entrenched and physical, mental and emotional energy suffers.

Symptoms of glucose intolerance can range from the mildly uncomfortable to the severely debilitating. Dr Carl Pfeiffer has classified glucose intolerance as one of the five main underlying factors in schizophrenia. Psychiatric symptoms of glucose intolerance have been noted to include unsocial or anti–social behaviour, phobias, suicide attempts, nervous breakdown and psychosis. In addition, studies have implicated sugar as a factor in the following conditions connected with mental and emotional health: aggressive behaviour [11,21,22,24,25,27], anxiety, attention–deficit [20] and hyperactivity, depression[13], eating disorders [15], fatigue [13], learning disabilities [14,16,18,23] and PMS. Caffeine has been implicated in fatigue [13], anxiety [12,26], depression [13], PMS, insomnia [13,17] psychotic episode and increased psychotic symptoms in schizophrenics [19].

Practical advice centering around nutritional support for the sufferer is certainly needed. The emphasis is on a core diet of complex carbohydrates, with adequate protein, low in saturated fat but rich in the essential fats and with plenty of water.

While complex carbohydrate foods, such as wholegrains or beans, release their sugar content slowly, not all simple carbohydrates are fast releasing. Most fruit contains a different kind of sugar, fructose, which is also slow releasing. Increasing 'slow releasing' sugar foods, (in the 'low' category in Chart 3 opposite) and reducing or avoiding 'fast releasing' sugar foods (in the 'high' category in Chart 3 opposite) and stimulants rapidly corrects glucose intolerance. Frequent meals and regular exercise also help to regulate glucose control. The micronutrients are crucial for carbohydrate metabolism. The B complex vitamins and vitamin C together with the minerals chromium, magnesium, zinc and manganese have been used therapeutically with great success. However, for those people caught up in mental or emotional difficulties, attention to diet can often come way down on a list of priorities. And for those glucose–intolerant people leaving wards and re–entering society alone, nutritional support alongside social support systems, needs to be given the recognition it deserves.

Anti–Nutrients

Anne spent much of her late teens in hospital due to severe manic-depression. During her manic phases she became violent, and then suffered suicidal depression. She was given lithium and chlorpromazine drug treatment. She gained weight and lost touch with those around her.

Then she consulted a nutrition counsellor. Tests revealed very high levels of copper and deficiencies of key brain nutrients. Once on a nutrition programme designed to detoxify the copper and correct imbalancess she became increasingly lucid, healthier and happier, as well as losing weight. At three monthly intervals she approached her psychiatrist to reduce her drugs, yet every time he refused. Of her own volution, she reduced all meedication over a year. Now she is drug-free and feels like a completely different person.

Since our bodies, brains and nervous systems are literally made from what we take in – through food, air and water – there is every reason to consider that changes in diet, pollution and environment could have a bearing on physical and mental health. The effects of recreational drugs like alcohol, or prescription drugs like anti–depressants illustrate the powerful influence of chemicals on mood and behaviour.

In the last 50 years alone, 3,500 new chemicals have been added to food. A further 3,000 have been introduced into our homes [8]. Heavy metals like lead and cadmium are so commonplace in a 20th century environment that the average person has 1,000 times (check) higher body levels than our ancestors [28]. Most of our food is sprayed with pesticides and herbicides such that the average person may have up to a gallon sprayed on the fruit and vegetables they consume in a year [29].

All of these are classified as anti–nutrients – substances that interfere either with our ability to absorb or to use essential nutrients, and in some cases, promote the loss of essential nutrients from the body.

Nobody really knows to what extent this modern cocktail of anti–nutrients messes up our mental health, however we do know that high intakes of lead, cadmium, certain food colourings and other chemicals can have a disastrous effect on intellectual performance and behaviour.

A high intake of anti–nutrients has been associated with mood swings, poor impulse control and aggressive behaviour, poor attention span, depression and apathy, disturbed sleep patterns, impaired memory and

ANTI-NUTRIENT	EFFECT	SOURCE	ANTAGONIST
Lead	Hyperactivity, aggression	Exhaust fumes	Vitamin C, Zinc
Cadmium	Aggression, confusion	Cigarettes	Vitamin C, Zinc
Mercury	Headaches, memory loss	Pesticides, fillings	Selenium
Aluminium	Associated with senility	Cookware, water	Zinc, Magnesium
Copper	Anxiety and phobia	Water	Zinc
Tartrazine	Hyperactivity	Food colourings	Zinc

intellectual performance. If these kinds of symptoms are present, the nutritional approach to promoting mental health includes testing for high levels of anti–nutrients and, if found, removing the source and detoxifying the body. Here are some examples of anti–nutrients, their source, effects in excess on mental health, and nutritional antagonists which help to lower body levels of these unwanted substances.

A nutrition counsellor can test for the presence of many of these anti–nutrients and devise a lifestyle, diet and supplement programme to eliminate this potential contributor to mental instability. The consequence of decreasing the burden of these anti-nutrients is a greater ability to cope with the unavoidable stresses life gives us to deal with.

Nutrients

Liz started suffering from depression at the age of 14. By the time she was 17 she had become extremely anxious, fearful and depressed and was hearing voices. She was put on three drugs - Sulpiride and Depixol injections, plus Kemadrin to offset the side-effects of the other drugs. The drugs somewhat sedated her but she continued to suffer from extreme depression and anxiety and continued to hear voices in her head. She also had psychotherapy but neither this, nor the drugs made any real difference.

She consulted a nutrition counsellor who identified chronic nutritional deficiencies and an excessive level of histamine, an neurotransmitter that affects the brain. Within six months she was no longer depressed, and rarely heard voices or became anxious. She came off all medication and continued to improve. She is now perfectly healthy and happy and recently gave birth to a baby girl. She experienced no post-natal depression.

The one major difference between mankind and virtually every other animal is the relatively large size of our brain in relation to body size. We humans have a brain ten times larger in relation to body size than virtually all animals. There are also chemical differences too, in that our brains have very high concentrations of certain essential nutrients and their derivatives. In fact, during early brain development, no less than half of all nutrients a fetus and young infant receives goes towards brain development.

Scientists have asked why we have these differences and how the brain could have developed in this way. There is now growing evidence that our distant ancestors may have specialised in exploiting a particularly nutrient–rich environment – the waters edge. During early primate evolution we may have lived in swampland and wetlands, eating highly nutritious seafood, shellfish, eggs and vegetation growing in the richest soil, nourished by mineral–rich waters 30. This optimum nutrition may have provided the raw materials to allow the brain and nervous system of primates to develop their complexity.

History aside, the fact is that our mental function is totally dependent on a daily basis on receiving a whole host of micro–nutrients, substances like vitamins, minerals and essential fatty acids, that are present in a healthy diet. B vitamins, for example, are needed by every single cell. A long–term deficiency is a known cause of severe mental illness. A short–term deficiency is associated with poor intellectual and behavioural performance. Recently, a series of studies have demonstrated that even adding small amounts of nutrients to the diets of ordinary school children can, for some, have a major effects on their intellectual performance [31].

Even back in the 1960s Drs. Hoffer and Osmond were able to demonstrate that so–called schizophrenics could be effectively treated with much larger amounts of vitamin B3 and vitamin C than could be achieved through diet alone [32]. Dr Carl Pfeiffer at the Brain Bio Center in New Jersey USA later identified the role of vitamin B6 and the mineral zinc in mental illness [33]. Now we know that deficiencies in magnesium, manganese, B12 and folic acid, as well as zinc and B6 can result in mental illness [34, 35, 36].

Of course, many people live under the illusion that as long as you eat a well balanced diet you get all the nutrients you need and assume that, however important these nutrients may be, they couldn't possibly be deficient.

Myth Of The Well Balanced Diet

The greatest lie in health care today is that "as long as you eat a well balanced diet you get all the nutrients you need". This is a lie because no single piece of research in the last decade has managed to show that people who consider themselves to be eating a well-balanced diet are receiving all the Recommended Daily Amounts (RDA) of vitamins and minerals, let alone those levels of nutrients that are consistent with optimum nutrition. The reality is that the vast majority of us are deficient in a number of essential nutrients, which include vitamins, minerals, essential fatty acids, and amino acids, the constituents of protein. Deficient, means 'not efficient', in other words that you are not functioning as efficiently as you could because you have an inadequate intake of one or more nutrients. If this comes as a shock consider the following facts.

● The average person in Britain in 1993, according to the National Food Survey, eats less than the EC RDA of 8 out of 13 nutrients for which RDAs exist. The average intake of zinc is 7.9mg, almost half the Recommended Daily Allowance of 15mg [37].

● RDA levels vary from country to country. A five-fold variation from is not at all uncommon. In other words scientists can't agree what we need.

● RDA's are not optimum. According to the National Academy of Sciences, who set US RDA's, "RDA's are neither minimal requirements nor necessarily optimal levels of intake" [38]. In the UK, government funds research to define the optimum intake of vitamins C and E to protect against cancer and heart disease, in recognition of the fact that RDA levels are not necessarily optimum [39]. Factors considered to raise one's requirements considerably above RDA levels include alcohol consumption, smoking, exercise habits, pregnancy, times of stress including puberty and premenstrual phases, pollution, and special dietary habits, for example vegetarianism. Suggested Optimal Nutrient Allowances (SONAs) are often 10 times higher than RDA levels40.

● There are 45 known essential nutrients. EC RDAs exist for only 13 of these.

● Food does not contain what you think it contains. Most of these surveys are based on recording what people eat and looking up what those foods contain in standard text books. But do they take into account that an orange can contain anything from 180mg of vitamin C to nothing41? A 100g serving of spinach can contain from 158mg of iron to 0.1mg depending on where it's grown. Carrots, that reliable source of vitamin A, can provide a massive 18,500ius down to a mere 70ius. Store an orange for two weeks and its vitamin C content will be halved. Boil a vegetable for 20 minutes and 50 per cent of its B vitamins will be gone [42]. Refine brown flour to make white and 78 per cent of the zinc, chromium and manganese are lost [43]. Today's food is not a reliable source of vitamins and minerals.

Essential Nutrients For Mental Health

The reality is that many people are deficient in essential brain nutrients and suffer from mental imbalance as a result. A nutritional approach to mental illness involves working out an individual's nutritional status and correcting any potential deficiency with diet and supplements. Much higher levels of nutrients are often needed to restore mental health than are needed to maintain it. There may also be some people who, perhaps for genetic reasons, need higher levels of nutrients than others to maintain mental health. Here are some of the key brain nutrients, the symptoms that occur in deficiency, and the best foods to eat.

NUTRIENT	EFFECTS OF DEFICIENCY	FOOD SOURCES
B3	Depression, psychosis	Wholegrains, vegetables
B6	Irritability, poor memory	Wholegrains, bananas
Folic Acid	Anxiety, depression	Green leafy vegetables
B12	Confusion, poor memory	Cheese, eggs
Zinc	Confusion, blank mind, apathy	Oysters, nuts, seeds, fish
Magnesium	Irritability, insomnia, depression	Vegetables, nuts, seeds
Manganese	Dizziness, convulsions	Nuts, seeds, tropical fruit

Brain Food

Most drugs currently being used to treat mental illness are designed to enhance or block the chemical messengers, called neurotransmitters, that allow information to flow in the brain. These neurotransmitters are themselves made from nutrients in food. For example, serotonin, the neurotransmitter that induces sleep, is made from an amino acid, tryptophan. The body also needs vitamin B3, B6 and iron to produce serotonin. Instead of giving drugs that block or enhance such neurotransmitters, nutrition counsellors often recommend specific nutrients to supply the raw materials the brain needs to rebalance neurotransmitters. Such approaches are much safer since these essential nutrients are much less toxic and less expensive than drugs, and are proving to be as effective, if not more so, in the treatment of certain kinds of mental health problems.

Food Allergy and Intolerance

Janet was diagnosed with manic depression at the age of 15. At times she would become completely hyperactive and manic, and at other times become completely depressed. She was put on three drugs - Lithium, Tegretol and Zirtek. These helped control the severity of her manic phases, but she was still frequently depressed and anxious.

Two years later she consulted a nutrition counsellor who found she was deficient in many nutrients, especially zinc, and allergic to wheat. As soon as her nutrient deficiencies were corrected and she stopped eating wheat her health rapidly improved. She was able to stop all medication and, provided she stays off wheat, no longer gets depressed. She is now doing her final degree exams and continues to feel good and achieve well. However, if she has any wheat, even inadvertently in a sauce, she becomes depressed, confused, forgetful and anxious for 3 to 4 days. Her manic phases, however, have never returned.

The knowledge that allergy to foods and chemicals can adversely affect moods and behaviour in susceptible individuals has been known for a very long time. Early reports, as well as current research, have found that allergies can affect any system of the body, including the central nervous system. They can cause a diversity of symptoms including fatigue, slowed thought processes, irritability, agitation, aggressive behaviour, nervousness, anxiety, depression, schizophrenia, hyperactivity and varied learning disabilities [44-51].

Allergic intolerance in susceptible individuals can be caused by a variety of substances. However, many people have reactions to various foods and chemicals.

The most convincing evidence that this is indeed so, comes from a well conducted double–blind, placebo controlled crossover trial by Dr Egger and his team who studied 76 hyperactive children to find out whether diet can contribute to behavioural disorders. The results showed that 79% of the children tested reacted adversely to artificial food colourants and preservatives, primarily to tartrazine and benzoic acid, which produced a marked deterioration in their behaviour.

However no child reacted to these alone. In fact 48 different foods were found to produce symptoms among the children tested. For example 64% reacted to cow's milk, 59% to chocolate, 49% to wheat, 45% to oranges,

39% to eggs, 32% to peanuts, and 16% to sugar. Interestingly enough it was not only the children's behaviour which improved after the individual dietary modification. Most of the associated symptoms also improved considerably, such as headaches, fits, abdominal discomfort, chronic rhinitis, aches in limbs, skin rashes and mouth ulcers 52.

Another similar double–blind controlled food trial by Dr Egger and his team was conducted on 88 children suffering from frequent migraines. As before, most children reacted to several foods and chemicals. However the following foods and chemicals were found to be most prevalent: cows milk provoked symptoms in 27 children, egg in 24, chocolate in 22, both oranges and wheat in 21, benzoic acid in 14 and tartrazine in 12.

Yet again, interestingly enough, after dietary modification, not only migraine improved but also associated physical disorders such as abdominal pain, muscle aches, fits, rhinitis, recurrent mouth ulcers, asthma, eczema, as well as a variety of behavioural disorders 53.

Adults are also affected by food and chemical allergy. When Dr Philpott, a US allergy expert, examined 250 emotionally disturbed patients for a possible presence of food or chemical allergies, using elimination and challenge diet, where specific foods and chemicals are first eliminated for a period of time and then carefully re-introduced, he found that the highest percentage of symptoms seemed to occur in patients diagnosed as psychotic. For example, out of 53 patients diagnosed as schizophrenic, 64% reacted adversely to wheat, 50% to cow's milk, 75% to tobacco and 30% to petrochemical hydrocarbons. The emotional symptoms caused by allergic intolerance ranged from mild central nervous system symptoms such as dizziness, blurred vision, anxiety, depression, tension, hyperactivity and speech difficulties to gross psychotic symptoms. At the same time, the individuals also experienced various adverse physical symptoms such as headaches, feeling of unsteadiness, weakness, palpitations and muscle aches and pains.

These studies are prime examples of how problems created by allergies often produce a multitude of physical and mental symptoms and affect many body systems. They not only can affect the central nervous system and the brain, but also usually affect the whole body in various ways. Furthermore these allergies are very specific for each individual, i.e. the same foods or chemicals hardly ever produce the same symptoms in different people. Therefore the diagnosis can only be made individually by using an elimination and challenge diet. If reactions occur, the diagnosis is positive. It should be noted that this test should always be done under expert supervision, particularly if symptoms include epileptic fits, asthma, schizophrenia or severe depression.

Here are a few examples of how this elimination and challenge diet have been used safely and effectively in treating people suffering from various mental health problems [52]

Study 1

Thirty patients suffering from anxiety, depression, confusion or difficulty in concentration were tested, using a placebo controlled trial, as to whether individual food allergies could really produce mental symptoms in these individuals. The results showed that allergies alone, not placebos, were able to produce the following symptoms: severe depression, nervousness, feeling of anger without a particular object, loss of motivation and severe mental blankness. The foods/chemicals which produced most severe mental reactions were wheat, milk, cane sugar, tobacco smoke and eggs [53].

Study 2

Ninety-six patients diagnosed as suffering from alcohol dependence, major depressive disorders and schizophrenia were compared to 62 control subjects selected from adult hospital staff members for a possible food or chemical intolerance. The results showed that the group of patients diagnosed as depressives had the highest number of allergies, i.e. 80% were found to be allergic to barley and 100% were allergic to egg white. Over 50% of alcoholics tested were found to be allergic to egg white, milk, rye and barley. Out of the group of people diagnosed as schizophrenics 80% were found to be allergic to both milk and eggs. Only 9% of the control group were found to suffer from any allergies [54].

Study 3

Routinely treated schizophrenics, who on admission were randomly assigned to a diet free of cereal grain and milk while on the locked ward, were discharged from the hospital about twice as rapidly as control patients assigned to a high–cereal diet. Wheat gluten secretly added to the cereal–free diet abolished this effect, suggesting that wheat gluten may be a cause of schizophrenic symptoms in susceptible individuals [55].

Two recent reports estimate that 2 in every 10 people now suffer from allergies [56,57]. The young developing nervous system seems to be particularly vulnerable to any allergenic or toxic overload, leading frequently to various behavioural disorders such as hyperactivity and learning disabilities. A further survey estimates that at least 1 child in 10 may react adversely to some common foods and food additives [58].

It is an interesting fact that a great number of drugs used in today's psychiatry are very similar in composition to antihistamines, which are commonly used in the treatment of allergies. For example tricyclic and related antidepressant drugs, such as imipramine (Tofranil) and Amitriptyline are also known to suppress brain histamine receptors. In addition, the following drugs used in the treatment of psychosis and related disorders are also known to inhibit brain histamine production: phenothiazine derivatives, such as chlorpromazine (Largactil), promazine (Sparine), Thioridazine etc. Furthermore promethazine, which is used in the treatment of anxiety and related disorders, is also commonly used in the treatment of allergies [59]. The fact that antihistamine-like drugs are widely used in the treatment of various mental disorders suggests that some mental problems could indeed be allergenic in origin. This being the case, it would surely be prudent to suggest that, before any medication is prescribed, all individuals suffering from mental health conditions should always be screened for a possible food or chemical intolerance.

PART THREE

Action Plan

The nutritional approach to mental illness is more 'labour intensive' than taking prescribed drugs. It requires gradual changes to lifelong habits. For this reason proper professional support from a nutrition counsellor, backed up by support and encouragement from family and friends, is essential. Nutrition counsellors are trained to identify if a person has allergies, glucose intolerance, nutrient deficiencies or anti-nutrient excesses. A lot of time can be saved by getting an accurate diagnosis. For these reasons we recommend you consult a nutrition counsellor (see How to Get Help).

In the meantime here are some simple steps anyone can take to promote mental and emotional health:

1 Cut down your intake of sugar and refined foods.

2 Eat more fresh fruit and whole foods (e.g seeds, nuts, beans, lentils, wholegrains)

3 Cut down your intake of stimulants - tea, coffee, chocolate, cola drinks, cigarettes.

4 Cut down your intake of alcohol.

5 Cut down your pollution load by reducing your time spent in smoky, high exhaust fume areas, and reducing cigarettes if you smoke.

6 Supplement your diet with a high strength multivitamin and mineral supplement containing C and B vitamins, as well as zinc, magnesium, manganese and chromium.

7 If your diet contains a lot of wheat (bread, pastries, wheat cereal, pasta) experiment with two weeks without wheat, eating oat cakes, rice cakes, corn or oat based cereals and buckwheat pasta instead. It is best to reintroduce a suspected allergen under the guidance of a nutrition counsellor.

8 If your diet contains a lot of milk products (milk, cheese, yoghurt etc.) experiment with two weeks without milk products, using soya milk instead. It is best to reintroduce a suspected allergen under the guidance of a nutrition counsellor.

Most habits take a month to break. So take one habit, like drinking coffee. Give yourself one month without it, then see how you feel. The healthier your diet the less will be the 'withdrawal' effects of these stimulants. The greater the withdrawal effects the worse this substance is for you. Take one step at a time and know that every step makes a difference.

How to Get Help

Help is widely available all over Britain. Many nutrition counsellors (sometimes called nutrition consultants, dietary therapists, dieticians or nutritionists) are available for guidance.

Most nutrition counsellors are in private practice and charge around £30 for an initial consultation which usually lasts for an hour. Some medical practices can refer you to a dietician on the NHS.

The Council for Nutrition Education and Therapy publish a nationwide Directory of Nutrition Counsellors. This is available for £2 (inc. p&p) from The Institute for Optimum Nutrition, Blades Court, Deodar Road, London SW15 2NU (Tel: 0181 877 9993 Fax: 0181 877 9980).

Some nutrition counsellors are more experienced than others in the field of mental health and nutrition so it is best to ask them if they can help you. If not, they can refer you to another nutrition counsellor who specialises in mental health problems.

In case of difficulty please contact the Institute for Optimum Nutrition which runs post-graduate courses in mental health and nutrition and can put you in touch with your nearest suitably qualified nutrition counsellor.

References

Who suffers?

1. Thompson D, The Mental Health Foundation.
    The Fundamental Facts. 1993
2. Gorman J, Mental Health Statistics. MIND Information Unit,
    December 1993

The Nutrition Connection

3. Jaffe R, Kruesi O,The Biochemical-Immunology Window: a Molecular View of
    Psychiatric Case Management. Int Clin Nut Rev 12, 1: 9-26, 1992
4. Osmond H, Hoffer A, Massive Niacin Treatment in Schizophrenia.
    The Lancet 316-320,10 February 1962
5. Pfeiffer C, The Schizophrenias. Biol Psych 2: 773-775, 1976
6. Werbach M, Nutritioanl Influences of Mental Illness. California,
    Third Line Press, 1991
7. Bryce-Smith D, Environmental and Chemical Influences on Behaviour and
    Mentation. Chem Soc Rev 15: 93-123, 1986 (John Jeyes lecture).
8. Davies S, Scientific and Ethical Foundations of Nutritional Medicine. Part 1 -
    Evolution, Adaptation and Health. J Nut Med 2, 3, 1991
9. King DS, Can Allergic Exposure Provoke Psychological Symptoms? A Double-
    Blind Test. Biol Psych 16(1):3-19, 1981 and Egger J et al, Controlled Trial of
    Oligoantigenic Treatment in the Hyperkinetic Syndrome. The Lancet, 540–545,
    March 9, 1985

Sugar & Stimulants

10. Virkkunen M, Reactive Hypoglycaemia Tendency Among Habitually Violent
    Offenders. Nut Rev 44: (May supp) 94-103, 1986
11. Benton D et al, Mild Hypoglycemia and Questionnaire Measures of
    Aggression. Biol Psychol l4 (1-2):129-35, 1982
12. Bruce M, Lader M, Caffeine Abstention in the Management of Anxiety
    Disorders. Psychol Med 19:211-14, 1989.
13. Christensen L, Psychological Distress and Diet - Effects of Sucrose and
    Caffeine. J Appl Nutr 40(1):44-50, 1988.
14. Colgan M ,Colgan L, Do Nutrient Supplements and Dietary Changes
    Affect Learning and Emotional Reactions of Children with Learning
    Difficulties? A Controlled Series of 16 Cases. Nutr Health 3.69 77,1904
15. Fullerton D et al,Sugar, Opionoids and Binge Eating.
    Brain Res Bull 14(6):673-80, 1985.
16. Goldman J et al, Behavioural Effects of Sucrose on Pre-School
    Children. J Abnormal Child Psychol 14(4):565-77, 1986
17. Karacan I et al, Dose-related Sleep Disturbances Induced by Coffee and
    Caffeine. Clin Pharmacol Ther 20:682-89, 1976
18. Lester M et al, Refined Carbohydrate Intake, Hair Cadmium Levels and
    Cognitive Functioning in Children. Nutr Behav 1:3-13, 1982.
19. Mikkelsen E, Caffeine and Schizophrenia. Behavioural Med. December 1980
20. PrinzR, Riddle D, Associations Between Nutrition and Behaviour in 5
    Year Old Children. Nutr Rev 43:Suppl, 1986
21. Roy A et al, Monamines, Glucose Metabolism, Aggression Toward Self
    and Others. Int J Neurosci 41(3-4):261-4, 1988

22.	Schauss A, Diet, Crime and Delinquency. Berkeley, California. Parker House, 1980

23.	Schoenthaler S et al, The Impact of a Low Food Additive and Sucrose Diet on Academic Performance in 803 New York City Public Schools. Int J Biosocial Res 8(2):185-95, 1986

24.	Virkkunen M, Reactive Hypoglycaemic Tendency Among Arsonists. Acta Psychiatr Scand 69(5):445-52, 1984

25.	Virkkkunen M,NarvanenS, Plasma Insulin, Tryptophan and Serotonin Levels During the Glucose Tolerance Test Among Habitually Violent and Impulsive Offenders. Neuropsychobiology 17(1-2):19-23,1987

26.	Wendel W, Beebe W, Glycolytic Activity in Schizophrenia. In: Orthomol Psychiatry,Treatment of Schizophrenia. Eds:Hawkins D, Pauling L, 1973

27.	Yaryura-Tobias J, Neziroglu F, Violent Behaviour, Brain Dysrythmia and Glucose Dysfunction. A New Syndrome . J Ortho Psych 4:182-5,1975

Anti–Nutrients

28.	Patterson C, An Alternative Perspective-Lead Pollution in the Environment. In Lead in the Human Environment, 265-349. Commission of Natural Resources Research Council, Washington DC, National Academy of Sciences, 1980

29.	Friends of the Earth Briefing Sheet: Pesticides. Pesticides Campaign, 26-28 Underwood St. London N1 7JQ, 1987

Nutrients

30.	The Aquatic Ape - selected papers, Nutrition & Health 9, 3, 1994

31.	Benton D, Roberts G, Effect of Vitamin and Mineral Supplementation on Intelligence of a Sample of School Children. The Lancet, Jan 23, 1988

32.	Osmond H, Hoffer A, Massive Niacin Treatment in Schizophrenia. The Lancet 316-320, 10 Feb, 1962

33.	Pfeiffer C et al, Treatment of Pyroluric Schizophrenia with Large Doses of Pyridoxine and Zinc. J Ortho Psych 3: 292-300, 1974

34.	Pfeiffer C, Bacchi D, Copper, Zinc, Manganese, Niacin and Pyridoxine in the Schizophrenias. J App Nut 27: 9-39, 1975

35.	Pliszka S, Rogeness G, Calcium and Magnesium in Children with Schizophrenia and Major Depression. Biol Psychiatry 19:871-876,1994

36.	Godfrey P et al, Lancet, 1990; 336: 392-5

37.	The Vitamin Scandal, Optimum Nutrition 7.3:4, 1994

38.	Nat Acad of Sciences. Recommended Dietary Allowances, 10th ed. USA, National Academy Press, 1990

39.	MAFF Funds Research To Define Optimum Intakes of Vitamin C and E. Optimum Nutrition 4.3: 5, 1991

40.	What is Optimum? Optimum Nutrition 7. 2: 46-47, 1994 & Suggested Optimal Nutrient Allowances, Cheraskin & Ringsdorf

41.	Colgan M, Your Personal Vitamin Profile. Blond & Briggs, 1983

42.	Holford P, What's Cooking. Optimum Nut rtion 5.3: 22-27, 1992,

43.	Mervyn L, Lecture on Mineral Losses at ION, unpublished data.

Allergies

44.   Randolph T, Allergy as a Causative Factor of Fatigue, Irritability and
      Behaviour Problems of Children. J Pediatr 31:560, 1947

45.   Rowe A, Allergic Toxemia and Fatigue. Ann Allergy 17:9, 1959

46.   Speer F, Etiology: Foods. In: Allergy of the Nervous System. Ed:Speer F,
      Springfield, Ill,Charles Thomas, 1970

47.   Campbell M, Neurologic Manifestations of Allergic Disease. Ann Allergy 31:485 1973

48.   Hall K, Allergy of the Nervous System: A Review. Annals of Allergy 36:49–64, 1976

49.   Pippere V, Some Varieties of Food Intolerance in Psychiatric Patients. Nutr Health
      3(3):125–136, 1984

50.   Pfeiffer C, Holford P Mental Illness and Schizophrenia:The Nutrition Connection.
      Thorsons, 1989

51.   Tuormaa T, An Alternative to Psychiatry. The Book Guild, 1991

52.   Egger et al, Controlled Trial of Oligoantigenic Treatment in the Hyperkinetic
      Syndrome, The Lancet 540–545, March 9,1985

53.   Egger J et al, Is Migraine a Food Allergy? A Double–Blind Controlled Trial of
      Oligoantigenic Diet Treatment.The Lancet 865–869, October 15, 1983

54.   Feingold B, Dietary Management of Behavior and Learning Disabilities.
      In: Nutrition and Behavior. Ed: SA Miller, p.37 Franklin Institute Press,
      Philadelphia, Pennsylvania, USA, 1981

55.   McGovern J et al. Ann Allergy 47:123, 1981

56.   Young E et al, A Population Study of Food Intolerance. The Lancet 343:1127-1129, 1994

57.   Effective Allergy Practice. British Society for Allergy & Environmental Medicine, 1984

58.   Adverse Reactions to Food, Topical Update, 2, National Dairy Council, 5-7 John Princes
      Street, London W1M OAP 1994

59.   Kanoff P, Greenland P, Brain Histamine Receptors as Targets for Anti-Depressant Drugs.
      Nature 272: 329-333, 1978

The majority of papers and publications referred to are to be found in the Lamberts Library at the Institute for Optimum Nutrition, Blades Court, Deodar Road, London SW15 2NU Tel: 0181 877 9993

Useful Reading

Mental Health & Mental Illness - The Nutrition Connection,
Pfeiffer C and Holford P, ION Press, 1995

Mental and Elemental Nutrients, *Pfeiffer C.* Keats Publishing Inc., 1975

An Alternative to Psychiatry, *Tuorma T,* The Book Guild,1991

Nutritional Influences on Mental Illness, *Werbach M,*
Third Line Press, 1991

Allergy and Nutrition Revolution, *Braly J,* Keats, 1992

All these books are available from ION, Blades Court, Deodar Road, London SW15 2NU. Please call 081-877 9993 for current price list.

How To Obtain More Copies Of This Book

Mental Ilness - The Nutrition Connection is a not-for-profit publication. All income received goes back into the Mental Health Project which exists to inform the public about the role of nutrition in mental health, to promote the nutrition connection to health professionals, policy makers and sufferers, and to provide resources to encourage more research and implementation of nutritional strategies to reduce mental suffering.

The best way to support this project is to buy copies of this book and circulate them key people such as your local GPs, MP, practitioners, health clinics, sufferers, relatives of sufferers and local health food shop. We also welcome any donation of time or money to support our aims.

1 copy £1 plus 25p postage &package

5 copies £5 (free postage & package)

Please send me:

_____ copies of **Mental Illness - Not All in the Mind**

I enclose a donation of £ _____ to the Mental Health Project

I enclose £ _____ payable to the ION (Mental Health Project) Ltd

NAME: _____

ADDRESS: _____

_____ POST CODE: _____

DAYTIME TELEPHONE NUMBER: _____

Now send this to: ION(Mental Health Project), Blades Court, Deodar Road, London SW15 2NU Tel: 0181 877 9993 Fax: 0181 877 9980

How To Obtain More Copies Of This Book

Mental Ilness - The Nutrition Connection is a not-for-profit publication. All income received goes back into the Mental Health Project which exists to inform the public about the role of nutrition in mental health, to promote the nutrition connection to health professionals, policy makers and sufferers, and to provide resources to encourage more research and implementation of nutritional strategies to reduce mental suffering.

The best way to support this project is to buy copies of this book and circulate them key people such as your local GPs, MP, practitioners, health clinics, sufferers, relatives of sufferers and local health food shop. We also welcome any donation of time or money to support our aims.

1 copy £1 plus 25p postage &package

5 copies £5 (free postage & package)

Please send me:

———— copies of **Mental Illness - Not All in the Mind**

I enclose a donation of £ ————— to the Mental Health Project

I enclose £ ——— payable to the ION (Mental Health Project) Ltd

NAME: ————————————————————————

ADDRESS: ——————————————————————

——————————————— POST CODE: ——————

DAYTIME TELEPHONE NUMBER:

Now send this to: ION(Mental Health Project), Blades Court, Deodar Road, London SW15 2NU Tel: 0181 877 9993 Fax: 0181 877 9980